THE **TRAVELS OF** THE PROPHET **IBRAHIM** علیـه السلام

Quran Stories for Little Hearts

By
S A N I Y A S N A I N   K H A N

Goodword**kidz**
Helping you build a family of faith

2

Long long ago, about 4000 years ago, in the land of Iraq a child was born whose name was Ibrahim عليه السلام (or Abraham).

4

He was gracious, tender-hearted and pure in faith. Allah was pleased with him and made him His best friend.

When Ibrahim عليه السلام grew up, he became a great prophet, and preached the truth and Allah's message in his country. Later he travelled to Syria, Palestine and Egypt.

When a beautiful son was born to his wife, Hajar (or Hagar), Ibrahim ﷺ was ordered by Allah to travel towards what we now know as Makkah along with his wife and the little child, whose name was Ismail (or Ishmael). They all travelled for a long time till they reached a lonely, barren valley, near two small hills called Safa and Marwah.

The Prophet Ibrahim عليه السلام asked his wife to stay near one of the hills along with the baby Ismail, and started to go away. His wife protested, "Why are you leaving us alone here? Are you leaving us here to die?" But Ibrahim عليه السلام replied, "My Lord has commanded me to do this." Then Hajar, breathing a sigh of relief, said: "If Allah has ordered you to do so, then He will not let us die."

After a while, little Ismail began to cry becuse he was thirsty. But there was not a single drop of water to drink. Hajar ran helplessly from one hill to another, but there was no water, nor was there any human being nearby to give her any.

As the baby was crying desperately with thirst and the mother was running from one hill to another, Allah caused a miracle to take place — a spring gushed forth beneath the feet of Ismail عليه السلام.

When Hajar saw this from a distance, she shouted, "Zamzam"—the sound made by rushing water in the Babylonian language.

Hajar came running and gave some fresh spring water to the thirsty child to drink. And so his life was saved. This spring became famous later on and was called by the name of Zamzam.

Ismail ﷷ and his mother began to live in the valley and, because of the Zamzam spring, more people gradually came to settle there, slowly building up a small town, which was later called Makkah.

From time to time Ibrahim ﷺ would visit Makkah to meet his family, especially to see his young Ismail growing up in the beautiful surroundings of nature — in a new town in a lovely valley surrounded by hills, away from the crowded cities where the people at that time were mostly idol-worshippers.

The moral of this story is that believers who, despite their hardships, follow the path of Allah, will find that, Allah will remain with them and help them in miraculous ways, just as the child Ismail عليه السلام was saved by the miracle of the Zamzam spring.

Find Out More

To know more about the message and meaning of Allah's words, look up the following parts of the Quran which tell the story of the Prophet Ibrahim عليه السلام:

> *Surah Ibrahim* 14:36-41
> *Surah al-Ankabut* 29:26-27

عليه السلام *Alayhis Salam* 'May peace be upon him.'
The customary blessings on the prophets.